Discipleship
The Growing Christian's Lifestyle

JAMES & MARTHA REAPSOME

D0110863

Discipleship
PUBLISHED BY WATERBROOK PRESS
12265 Oracle Blvd., Suite 200
Colorado Springs, Colorado 80921
A division of Random House, Inc.

ISBN 0-87788-175-8

United States of America
2005

10 9 8 7 6 5 4 3

Contents

How to Use This Studyguide

Fisherman studyguides are based on the inductive approach to Bible study. Inductive study is discovery study; we discover what the Bible says as we ask questions about its content and search for answers. This is quite different from the process in which a teacher *tells* a group *about* the Bible—what it means and what to do about it. In inductive study, God speaks directly to each of us through his Word.

A group functions best when a leader keeps the discussion on target, but the leader is neither the teacher nor the "answer person." A leader's responsibility is to *ask*—not *tell.* The answers come from the text itself as group members examine, discuss, and think together about the passage.

There are four kinds of questions in each study. The first is an *approach question.* Asked and answered before the Bible passage is read, this question breaks the ice and helps you start thinking about the topic of the Bible study. It begins to reveal where thoughts and feelings need to be transformed by Scripture.

Some of the earlier questions in each study are *observation questions*—who, what, where, when, and how—designed to help you learn some basic facts about the passage of Scripture.

Once you know what the Bible says, you need to ask, *What does it mean?* These *interpretation questions* help you discover the writer's basic message.

Next come *application questions*, which ask, *What does it mean to me?* They challenge you to live out the Scripture's life-transforming message.

Fisherman studyguides provide spaces between questions for jotting down responses as well as any related questions you would like to raise in the group. Each group member should have a copy of the studyguide and may take a turn in leading the group.

A group should use any accurate, modern translation of the Bible such as the *New International Version,* the *New American Standard Bible,* the *New Living Translation,* the *New Revised Standard Version,* the *New Jerusalem Bible,* or the *Good News Bible.* (Other translations or paraphrases of the Bible may be referred to when additional help is needed.) Bible commentaries should not be brought to a Bible study because they tend to dampen discussion and keep people from thinking for themselves.

Suggestions for Group Leaders

1. Thoroughly read and study the Bible passage before the meeting. Get a firm grasp on its themes and begin applying its teachings for yourself. Pray that the Holy Spirit will "guide you into all truth" (John 16:13) so that your leadership will guide others.

2. If any of the studyguide's questions seem ambiguous or unnatural to you, rephrase them, feeling free to add others that seem necessary to bring out the meaning of a verse.

3. Begin (and end) the study promptly. Start by asking someone to pray that every participant will both understand the passage and be open to its transforming power. Remember, the Holy Spirit is the teacher, not you!

4. Ask for volunteers to read the passages aloud.

5. As you ask the studyguide's questions in sequence, encourage everyone to participate in the discussion. If some are silent, try gently suggesting, "Let's have an answer from someone who hasn't spoken up yet."

6. If a question comes up that you can't answer, don't be afraid to admit that you're baffled. Assign the topic as a research project for someone to report on next week, or say, "I'll do some studying and let you know what I find out."

7. Keep the discussion moving, but be sure it stays focused. Though a certain number of tangents are inevitable, you'll want to quickly bring the discussion back to the topic at hand. Also, learn to pace the discussion so that you finish the lesson in the time allotted.

8. Don't be afraid of silences; some questions take time to answer, and some people need time to gather courage to speak. If silence persists, rephrase your question, but resist the temptation to answer it yourself.

9. If someone comes up with an answer that is clearly illogical or unbiblical, ask for further clarification: "What verse suggests that to you?"

10. Discourage overuse of cross references. Learn all you can from the passage at hand, while selectively incorporating a few important references suggested in the studyguide.

11. Some questions are marked with a ✄ . This indicates that further information is available in the Leader's Notes at the back of the guide.

12. For further information on getting a new Bible study group started and keeping it functioning effectively, read *You Can Start a Bible Study Group* by Gladys Hunt and *Pilgrims in Progress: Growing Through Groups* by Jim and Carol Plueddemann. (Both books are available from Shaw Books).

Suggestions for Group Members

1. Learn and apply the following ground rules for effective Bible study. (If new members join the group later, review these guidelines with the whole group.)

2. Remember that your goal is to learn all that you can *from the Bible passage being studied.* Let it speak for itself without using Bible commentaries or other Bible passages. There is more than enough in each assigned passage to keep your group productively occupied for one session. Sticking to the passage saves the group from insecurity ("I don't have the right reference books—or the time to read anything else.") and confusion ("Where did *that* come from? I thought we were studying _____.").

3. Avoid the temptation to bring up those fascinating tangents that don't really grow out of the passage you are discussing. If the topic is of common interest, you can bring it up later in informal conversation after the study. Meanwhile, help one another stick to the subject.

4. Encourage one another to participate. People remember best what they discover and verbalize for

themselves. Some people are naturally shy, while others may be afraid of making a mistake. If your discussion is free and friendly and you show real interest in what other group members think and feel, the quieter ones will be more likely to speak up. Remember, the more people involved in a discussion, the richer it will be.

5. Guard yourself from answering too many questions or talking too much. Give others a chance to share their ideas. If you are one who participates easily, discipline yourself by counting to ten before you open your mouth.

6. Make personal, honest applications and commit yourself to letting God's Word change you.

The Growing Christian's Lifestyle

n a culture where individuality and "doing your own thing" are considered sacred rights, we still see many people desperately seeking someone or something to follow that will give their life meaning and structure. And there is no shortage of gurus and experts to follow these days: spiritual teachers, indulging therapists, fitness fanatics, political innovators, scientific theorists—take your pick. The choices we make about whom we admire, follow, and wish to emulate reveal much about who we are and who we want to be.

Those who follow Jesus and learn his way are called his *disciples*. Both the requirements for and the steps toward discipleship are laid out in various ways in Scripture. This studyguide is by no means exhaustive, nor is it meant to teach how to make disciples of other people. Rather, it is for groups or individuals who want to understand for themselves what it means to be Jesus' disciple today. We will examine several principles of discipleship and look at two New Testament personalities who demonstrate some essential characteristics of a disciple.

We pray that this studyguide will enable you to make new discoveries from the Bible, to understand their implications for your life, and to live out the changes the Holy Spirit impresses upon you to make. May you find true freedom as you learn to be more like Jesus, and may you follow with purpose the path he has laid before you.

Conditions for Being a Disciple

LUKE 14:16-33

F ollowing Jesus is not a matter of simple belief; it is a decision that will affect our worldview, our choices, our relationships, our entire life. Jesus welcomes everyone to follow him and insists that we seriously consider the cost of being his disciple. His requirements are the same today as they were two thousand years ago. In this study, you'll discover what Jesus expects of the person who follows him and what the conditions for discipleship are.

1. If you were a leader who intended to change the world, what kinds of people would you choose to be your closest friends and supporters?

READ LUKE 14:16-24.

2. What were the responses of the invited guests to the banquet invitation?

What did their excuses reveal about their attitudes toward the host?

3. What was the host's reaction to their excuses? Who ended up attending the banquet? Why?

4. The context of the passage suggests that Jesus was telling this parable to the religious elite—those who

considered themselves to be the friends of God and first in line for his favor. What do you think Jesus was saying to them?

READ LUKE 14:25-33.

5. According to verses 26-27 and 33, what three conditions did Jesus give for being his disciple?

✗ 6. Compare verse 26 with Exodus 20:12 and 1 Timothy 5:8. In light of these teachings, explain what Jesus meant when he called his followers to *hate* their families.

7. In Jesus' day, a cross was an instrument of execution—a means of death. What would it mean for a prospective disciple to be willing to carry his or her own cross?

8. The requirement in verse 33 concerns possessions. How might possessions hinder a person from becoming a disciple of Jesus?

9. What point was Jesus making in the two parables in verses 28-32?

10. Why is a hasty, emotional decision not a wise way to enlist as a disciple of Jesus? What is more important than an enthusiastic start?

11. Compare the excuses given in verses 18-20 with Jesus' conditions for discipleship in this later section. What contrasts do you see?

12. Of the conditions Jesus gave for being his disciple, which ones are hardest for you to meet at this point in your life? Why?

13. What counsel would you give a friend who says, "The conditions are too hard. I can't be a disciple. It just isn't worth it."?

Close in prayer, silently or aloud, thanking God for his invitation and confessing the ways you fall short of his conditions for discipleship.

The Disciple's Lord

COLOSSIANS 1:9-20

Jesus' conditions for being a disciple may seem demanding until we realize and understand who he really is. In this passage we are shown an amazing picture of who it is we are called to follow. The apostle Paul prayed for the faithful disciples of the Colossian church, and one of his requests was that they would grow in their knowledge of Jesus Christ. Not only do we see here an example of how to pray for other disciples, but we also get a glorious glimpse of the greatness of our Lord and Master.

1. List two or three adjectives you would use to describe who Jesus is to a non-Christian. Explain your choices.

✐ READ COLOSSIANS 1:9-20.

2. From the tone of Paul's prayer, describe his feelings for these disciples whom he had never met.

3. Rephrase each of the requests in verses 9-11 in your own words.

What do you learn about God from these requests?

✐ 4. When do you most feel that you are living a life worthy of and pleasing to the Lord?

5. What three strong verbs did Paul use to describe what God has done for the Colossian disciples (verses 12-13)?

In what ways are these actions of God evident in your own life?

6. Read verses 12-14 silently, inserting your name in each sentence. How would meditating on God's actions help you develop in the areas that Paul prayed for in verses 9-12 (wisdom, endurance, patience with joy, thankfulness)?

7. List as many facts as possible about the Son from verses 15-20. Begin each sentence with "Jesus...."

8. What is Jesus' relationship to nature in the past and in the present?

In what ways do the discoveries that are made through the use of microscopes and telescopes add to your appreciation of the things said about God in verses 16-17?

9. What is Jesus' relationship to authorities? How would an understanding of this relationship protect disciples from two extreme attitudes: rejecting authority or living in fear of authority?

10. What is Jesus' relationship to the church (verse 18)? How did he achieve this position?

11. What does it mean for Christ to be the image of the invisible God (verses 15,19)?

12. In addition to what we have already learned about God's work on our behalf, what further action is described in verse 20? What did it cost?

13. Reflect on all that God has done for you through Christ. What effect does remembering these things have on you when you feel proud? when you feel discouraged?

Spend time worshiping our pre-eminent Master, the Lord Jesus Christ. Pray for one another, using the requests in Paul's prayer.

The Disciple's Identity and Resources

1 Peter 1:22–2:10; 2 Timothy 3:14-17

B ecause human emotions, reactions, and limitations can distort how we see ourselves, we need a clear understanding of who we are from God's omnipotent point of view. When we remember who we were before we knew Christ and realize our new identity in him, we are free to love others. We don't need to compare ourselves with others or denigrate ourselves. Instead, we can encourage one another as we tap into the useful resources and power that Scripture provides.

1. If you were to draw a picture of how you think God sees you, what colors would you use? Explain.

Read 1 Peter 2:4-10.

2. In this passage believers are described as "living stones" (verse 5). What relationship do these living stones have to one another?

Why does this analogy rule out being a "lone-wolf disciple"—a person who doesn't think he or she needs anyone?

3. In what ways has the process of being built together with other "stones" sometimes been a painful experience for you? In what ways has it been a joyful experience?

4. List each of the titles given to disciples in verse 9. What does each title contribute to your understanding of who you and other disciples are?

🖋 5. According to verse 9, what is a disciple's purpose? How does this purpose affect the focus of a disciple's attention and priorities?

6. Contrast the past and present identities of the Christians Peter was addressing (verse 10). How does this contrast, which is true of all believers, influence your attitude toward God and yourself?

READ 1 PETER 1:22–2:3.

7. In what ways had the Word already affected these disciples (1:22-23)? In light of those changes, what were they commanded to do?

8. What do the contrasts in 1:23-25 add to your appreciation of God's Word?

9. Use a dictionary to define each of the sins the disciples were to rid themselves of.

Have you been tempted by any of these sins in your life? Which ones? How did you deal with them?

10.   How does Peter's description of who you are—not who you feel like—affect the following:

your self-esteem

your independent spirit

your response to criticism

READ 2 TIMOTHY 3:14-17.

🖉 11. What role did the Word of God have in Timothy's life?

12. Use a dictionary to define the ways Scripture is useful in our lives in the following areas:

teaching

rebuking

correcting

training

13. How is Scripture performing any of these actions in your life? Be specific.

14. If you want to grow spiritually (1 Peter 2:2) and be "thoroughly equipped for every good work" (2 Timothy 3:17), what changes in your attitude toward Scripture may be necessary?

What changes will you need to make in your schedule in order to be better equipped "for every good work" (verse 17)?

The Disciple's Standard of Greatness

MARK 10:32-45; JOHN 13:1-17

In 1948 Dr. Donald Gray Barnhouse spoke at the Keswick Convention in England. He surveyed the audience and said, "The way to up is down." That's hardly the way to begin a sermon. Then he said, "The way to down is up." Most of the audience thought he was a nut.

Jesus' disciples probably had a similar reaction to his upside-down teachings about who is first and who is last. The cultural view of greatness in Jesus' day was not much different from ours. But Jesus taught and exemplified an altogether different kind of greatness for his disciples to emulate.

1. Whom do you consider to be a "great" or important person? What makes him or her great?

READ MARK 10:32-45.

2. What emotions might Jesus have experienced as he related the details of what he would face in Jerusalem?

3. Contrast what Jesus had on his mind at this time with what James and John were thinking about.

4. Give contemporary examples of the kind of "greatness" Jesus described in verse 42.

✐ 5. What was Jesus' definition of greatness?

List some specific ways you can be someone's servant this week.

READ JOHN 13:1-17.

6. What did Jesus know about himself (verses 1-3)? In light of that knowledge, what did he do?

7. Why do you think the writer mentioned Jesus' thoughts before describing his actions?

8. What did Jesus' actions in verses 4-5 teach his disciples?

9. How does your self-image affect your ability to serve others?

10. How does serving others differ from being enslaved to everyone's demands and never being able to say no?

11. Why is God's view of greatness so hard for us to put into practice, while the world's view of greatness is so easy to understand and act out?

12. What can a disciple do when he or she feels pulled toward worldly greatness?

A Disciple:
John the Baptist

LUKE 3:1-20; JOHN 1:19-34; 3:22-30; MATTHEW 11:1-15

We are told that John wore clothes made of camel's hair, that he ate locusts and wild honey, and that he warned people incessantly to repent and be baptized. If you had been out by the Jordan River in the hot Judean desert to see John the Baptist, you might have wondered if this strange prophet was legitimate.

Although John the Baptist seemed a bit eccentric, crowds of people responded to his powerful message. John met the conditions of discipleship that we read about earlier in this studyguide. He recognized Jesus' identity, he understood his own identity, and he lived as a servant of God, willing to obey no matter what the cost.

1. From what you have heard or read up to this point, what impresses you most about John the Baptist?

READ LUKE 3:1-20.

2. What was John's message? According to verses 10-14, what actions would give evidence of repentance?

3. What did John understand about Christ? about himself?

4. What consequences did John suffer for rebuking Herod for his sin (verses 19-20)?

READ JOHN 1:19-34.

   ✐ 5. What words did John use to identify himself (verse 23)? Describe his sense of his own importance and responsibility.

   6. What new facts about Jesus did John give in this passage? In what way(s) did these facts accentuate the difference between John and Jesus?

READ JOHN 3:22-30.

   7. About what situation was John questioned by his disciples?

✐ 8. What perspective did John have concerning Jesus'
rising popularity? How do you think John felt about
the situation?

READ MATTHEW 11:1-15.

✐ 9. Why might John's circumstances and the news of
Jesus' activities cause John to have doubts about
Jesus' identity and prompt him to send his disciples
to question Jesus?

10. What comfort would John have found in the
answer Jesus sent back?

11. What did Jesus think about John and his service
(verses 9-11)?

12. John modeled Jesus' standard of greatness presented in Mark 10:42-45. He served people by insisting that they demonstrate their repentance by changed behavior. How can you confront others as a servant?

13. John understood who he was and who his Lord was. What do you learn from his example about how to:

handle doubts

set priorities

evaluate your own importance

The Disciple's Motivation and Message

2 CORINTHIANS 5:6-21

Our motivation to follow Christ and proclaim the Good News to others can often fluctuate. There is a danger that our journey of discipleship will turn into a lifeless routine, unless we are convinced of God's deep love for us and of the truth of the gospel. The gospel message excited the apostle Paul, and he was eager to preach it. In this study we will learn why he took his calling so seriously.

1. At this point in your life, what motivates you to follow Christ?

Read 2 Corinthians 5:6-21.

2. What were Paul's motives for preaching (verses 11,14)?

3. Paul's detractors were apparently accusing him of being crazy. Explain Paul's response (verse 13).

4. What two conclusions did Paul draw from the facts of Jesus' death and resurrection (verses 14-15)?

5. How had Paul's understanding of Jesus' death for everyone changed his way of looking at people?

6. List the verbs in verses 18-19 that tell what God has done. Discuss the meaning and significance of each one.

✗ 7. What feelings does the word *reconciled* carry with it? What responsibility is attached to being reconciled (verse 18)?

8. What is the content of the message of reconciliation? At whom is the message aimed?

9. What responsibilities and privileges does an ambassador have? In what way(s) did Paul show himself to be an ambassador?

10. What effect does the fear of God have on your behavior?

11. What effect has Christ's love had on your life?

12. Describe two responsibilities you will assume as a Christian ambassador who has been given the ministry of reconciliation.

13. What has this study shown you about what needs to change in your life?

Close in prayer, asking God to help you make the changes you need to make.

The Disciple's Values and Goals

PHILIPPIANS 3:1-16

A television crew on the streets of Chicago conducted a survey, asking passersby, "What matters most to you?" Some people indicated that their career was most important to them; others cited family members or friends. Some said their houses were very important, and some even answered, "Me!"

In this study we will look at the contrast between what Paul valued most before he became a disciple of Christ and after. Paul refuted Jewish Christians who were teaching the Philippians that they had to be circumcised—in keeping with Jewish law—to be fully accepted by God. He used some strong language to show us what does and doesn't matter in being a disciple of Jesus.

1. What goals do you have for your life? What do your goals reveal about what is most important to you?

Read Philippians 3:1-11.

2. Contrast physical circumcision with the true circumcision that Paul described in verse 3.

3. Contrast what Paul valued before becoming a disciple of Jesus with what he valued afterward (verses 5-9).

Give a modern parallel for each of the things Paul formerly put his confidence in.

4. After his conversion, what was Paul's only basis for being confident of God's acceptance?

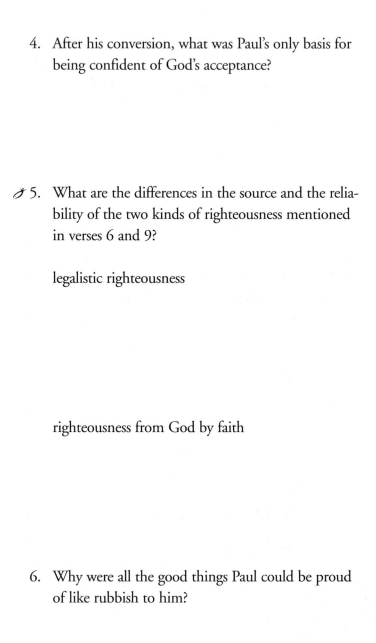 5. What are the differences in the source and the reliability of the two kinds of righteousness mentioned in verses 6 and 9?

legalistic righteousness

righteousness from God by faith

6. Why were all the good things Paul could be proud of like rubbish to him?

7. Review the conditions listed in Luke 14:26-27, 33 for being a disciple of Jesus. In what way(s) did Paul fulfill Jesus' requirements?

↗ 8. After Paul acquired a new value system, what goals did he set for himself (verses 10-11)? Briefly explain each one.

READ PHILIPPIANS 3:12-16.

9. We've seen that Paul had clearly defined goals. Why did he reject the idea that he had reached perfection and was free to live any way he liked?

10. In verses 12-14, Paul's words would bring to readers' minds the races that the Romans ran. How does picturing a runner in a race help you understand discipleship?

Why must a runner not look back?

11. What are some of the things that Paul considered "what is behind"? What are some of those things for you?

12. What is the disciple's role in his or her own continuing maturity? What is God's role (verses 15-16)?

13. What things are you tempted to value more than knowing Jesus Christ? What specific things can you do this week to "press on" toward the goals listed in verse 10?

In closing, pray that the Lord will help you "press on" toward what really matters. Ask each person to pray for the one on his or her right.

The Disciple's Inner Warfare

GALATIANS 5:16-26

As Christians, we can be our own worst enemies, and all too easily we succumb to sinful desires. Even a disciple who is motivated to be a follower and an ambassador of Jesus Christ and has set proper values and goals still fights an internal battle against sin. The Bible is realistic about this never-ending struggle. But it also reminds us that we have the power of the Holy Spirit on our side to help us in the struggle and to enable us to bear lasting fruit.

1. What do you do to resist and battle sin in your own life?

Read Galatians 5:16-26.

2. What are the two opposing forces in the Christian's inner warfare (verse 17)? In what way does a person choose to follow each one?

3. The acts of the sinful nature are listed in verses 19-21. What areas of life are included? What tells you that this is not an exhaustive list?

4. Discuss how the desires of the sinful nature work against the Spirit.

⊅ 5. Which acts of the sinful nature have you been tempted to tolerate as "not so bad"? How serious are all of them to God (verse 21)?

6. What are the Spirit's qualities called (verse 22)? What insight does that name give you about their origin and development?

7. What spiritual fruit has resulted from your walk with God?

⊅ 8. What light does verse 24 shed on the command in verse 16?

9. Because we, as disciples, are made alive by the Spirit, we are also to keep in step with the Spirit (verse 25). What does this guideline add to your understanding of our relationship to the Holy Spirit?

10. When facing daily issues that can mean either success or defeat in spiritual warfare, what basic choice must the disciple make to ensure victory? What can you do to make that choice?

11. God knows that, by themselves, disciples cannot win the war against their sinful nature. How can the work of the Holy Spirit make victory over sin a reality in a disciple's life?

⌒ 12. What tensions between living by the sinful nature and living by the Spirit did you face this week? What can you do to depend more on the Holy Spirit when you face these situations in the future?

The Disciple's Outer Struggles

SELECTIONS FROM 2 CORINTHIANS 4–12

L ife is no smooth and easy road for any of us. A quick look at the headlines or a brief talk with friends reminds us that just about everybody is having a hard time. The apostle Paul faced severe outward difficulties in his life—poor health, material insecurity, danger. Though the details differ, we all experience feelings of distress that accompany difficult times. In his second letter to the Corinthians, Paul shows us how he coped with this external warfare, and how God's grace is always present.

1. Have you ever experienced a difficult situation because of your faith? How did you handle it?

READ 2 CORINTHIANS 4:7-15.

2. What illustration did Paul use to describe the disciple and God's work in him or her? What is the significance of the words *treasure* and *jars of clay?*

3. Describe Paul's circumstances in verses 8-9. Why was he not destroyed by these experiences?

4. What good was coming out of these painful struggles in Paul's life?

READ 2 CORINTHIANS 4:16-18.

5. Instead of losing heart, what did Paul see happening to him?

What did Paul mean by "inwardly we are being renewed day by day" (verse 16)?

6. How do the words "we fix our eyes…on what is unseen" convey God's transcendence beyond our problems and all of life and its difficulties (verse 18)?

7. How did Paul compare his experience in the present with what was yet to come?

Read 2 Corinthians 6:3-10.

8. What outer struggles did Paul face? How would these struggles affect a person physically, spiritually, mentally, and emotionally?

9. What weapons of righteousness did Paul use in his struggles (verses 6-7)? Which of these weapons do you need to develop?

10. Verses 8-10 illustrate 2 Corinthians 4:18 by contrasting the seen and temporary with the unseen and eternal. What things *seemed* to be true in Paul's life? What was *really* true?

11. Describe a time in your life when you were sorrowful, yet rejoicing; poor, yet making many rich; having nothing, yet possessing everything.

Read 2 Corinthians 12:7-10.

12. Paul wrote about the lesson he learned from one of his hardest struggles. What was his problem? What purpose was it to accomplish?

13. What did Paul do about his problem? What did he receive instead of what he had requested?

14. What was Paul's attitude toward his outer struggles? What do you think made it possible for him to maintain that attitude?

15. What can you do to develop Paul's perspective on the outer struggles you face?

What spiritual weapons and resources can you draw on this week to help you in your struggles?

The Disciple's Responsibilities

ROMANS 12

Have personal devotions. Memorize Scripture. Witness often. Attend church. Tithe regularly. These are responsibilities we often urge new disciples to embrace for spiritual growth. And with good reason. But in this study, the apostle Paul goes deeper, defining a disciple's responsibilities as something more than activities or busyness. He focuses on who we are and how that expresses itself in right relationships and loving actions.

1. What's the difference between a "doing" faith and a "being" faith?

READ ROMANS 12:1-8.

𝄢 2. What commands did Paul give in verses 1-2?

What do you think is required of the body and the mind in order to obey these commands?

3. When we obey these commands, what can we learn about God's will?

𝄢 4. What protection do verses 3-8 give us from either overestimating or underestimating our true worth?

5. List the gifts disciples are to use in helping each other (verses 6-8). Which of these gifts have you had the opportunity to use? How?

READ ROMANS 12:9-21.

6. The commands in verses 9-21 describe specific responsibilities for believers. List the commands that pertain to:

your personal responsibilities

how you should treat other people

how you should respond to the world

7. Why does the disciple need the commands that relate to him- or herself?

8. As a study group of disciples, how well are you obeying these commands toward one another? Be specific.

How well are you following these commands in your church?

9. In verse 2, disciples are commanded not to be conformed to this world. Contrast the way world might handle conflict with the way disciples are to handle it (verses 14-21).

10. What opportunities do you have to practice any of these responsibilities?

11. The disciple's responsibilities are defined here in terms of right relationships and character rather than by activities and busyness. Look again at the commands in verses 13,15-16, and 20. How do these responsibilities reinforce Jesus' definition of greatness in Mark 10:43-45?

12. How would obeying the instructions in verses 1-2 help disciples in the internal warfare against sin and self?

How can obeying these instructions help disciples with outer struggles?

A Disciple: Barnabas

SELECTIONS FROM ACTS 4–15

It's one thing to study the qualities of discipleship. It's another thing to live them out. As you investigate the life of Barnabas, look for ways in which he lived out his faith, used his gifts, and exemplified characteristics of a disciple of Jesus Christ.

1. Think of someone you really look up to spiritually. Which of the discipleship qualities we have studied do you see evident in his or her life?

Read Acts 4:32-37.

2. What would have impressed you about this new church if you had been a citizen of Jerusalem?

3. What do you learn about Barnabas in this passage? Why do you think the apostles gave him his nick-name?

4. What evidence do you see in Barnabas's life that he met some of the requirements of discipleship? Compare with Mark 10:42-45 and Luke 14:25-33.

READ ACTS 9:26-30.

5. What was the church's initial reaction to Saul? Why did the Christians change their minds?

6. How do you suppose Barnabas knew the information about Saul that the others did not know?

In what ways did Barnabas live up to the meaning of his name given in Acts 4:36?

READ ACTS 11:19-30.

7. What new development occurred in the growth of the church?

8. Why did the Jerusalem church send Barnabas to Antioch? What were his qualifications for the job?

9. Why do you think Barnabas went to look for Saul? What does this tell you about him?

READ ACTS 13:1-5,13; 15:36-41.

10. Barnabas and Saul received a new assignment (13:1-5). According to verse 5, what was the role of John Mark, Barnabas's cousin?

11. What difference of opinion arose between Barnabas and Paul (15:36-41)?

In what way was Barnabas's attitude toward John Mark consistent with his character?

12. In what way(s) did Barnabas fulfill almost all of the responsibilities given in Romans 12?

What part of Barnabas's example can you follow this week?

13. When Paul emerged as a leader, what sins listed in Galatians 5:20-21 might have tempted Barnabas?

How would the qualities attributed to him in Acts 11:24 have enabled him to resist those temptations?

14.   What character qualities do you want God to build into your life to help you overcome jealousy, envy, selfishness, anger, dissension, or strife?

The Disciple's Basic Requirement

JOHN 21:15-22; 15:9-15

It's a tall order: loving God above all else, counting the cost, knowing our identity, leaning on the Scriptures, serving with humility, being an ambassador of reconciliation, winning the battles against sin and circumstances, setting goals, and renewing our mind. We can easily feel overwhelmed by what it really means to be a disciple of Christ.

But underneath all of these requirements for discipleship is simply a desire to follow Christ—to walk with our Lord, to go in his direction. We don't have to do it perfectly, just steadfastly. And as we trust his love and live our lives in the power of the Holy Spirit, we will come to know the joy of remaining in him.

1. Of the list of requirements for discipleship that we have studied, which ones do you anticipate will be hardest for you to put into practice? Why?

READ JOHN 21:15-22.

⚯ 2. Peter had denied Jesus three times prior to the Cru-
    cifixion. If you had been Jesus, what question might
    you have asked Peter at this time?

    What question did Jesus ask Peter? Why do you
    think he repeated it three times?

3. What do you think Jesus meant by "more than
    these" (verse 15)?

4. On what basis did Jesus give this repentant disciple
    new responsibilities?

What would it mean for Peter to feed and tend Jesus' sheep?

5. What did Jesus say in response to the concern Peter expressed in verse 21?

What was the key issue for Peter to remember?

6. When we disappoint ourselves and the Lord, why is our love for Jesus the basis for a fresh start?

READ JOHN 15:9-15.

7. Jesus gave a standard by which we can clearly evaluate whether or not we really love him. Instead of wondering if we feel love, what objective measure can we use to know if we are abiding in Jesus' love?

8. Why do you think Jesus made our love for others the test of our love for him?

9. What is the difference between a friend and a servant?

What difference does it make to you that Jesus wants his disciples to be his friends, not just his servants?

10. Why is your heart motive more important to Jesus than your pledge of great performance or your promises to do better?

11. Write out some goals for your continuing journey of following after Jesus. What can you do to better allow God to help you achieve them?

End in prayer, surrendering your goals to Jesus and giving him control of each step as you follow him.

Leader's Notes

Study 1: Conditions for Being a Disciple

Question 4. "It has been suggested that the parable was deliberately modeled by Jesus on a Jewish story of a *nouveau riche* tax collector who tried to gain social standing among the aristocrats by inviting them to dinner but was harshly rebuffed by them. The upper-class audience addressed by Jesus would have thoroughly appreciated the story—until it was borne in upon them that this was how they were treating God's invitation given to them by Jesus" (J. G. Baldwin, *The New Bible Commentary: Revised,* Grand Rapids: Eerdmans, 1970, p. 911).

Question 6. The *Good News Bible* translates Luke 14:26, "Whoever comes to me cannot be my disciple unless he loves me more than he loves his father and his mother, his wife and his children, his brothers and his sisters, and himself as well." Manley and Oldham supply the note: "Hate, i.e., love less than Me, especially if there should be a conflict between their claims and Mine" (*Search the Scriptures,* Downers Grove, Ill.: Inter-Varsity, 1949, p. 30).

Study 2: The Disciple's Lord

Note on Colossians 1:9-20. If possible, read this passage aloud from several translations.

Question 4. According to *The American Heritage Dictionary, worthy* means "having worth, merit, or value; useful or valu-

able; having sufficient worth; deserving." Keep these defini-
tions in mind as you answer this question.

Question 7. "The term *first-born* is commonly used to mean
'supreme' or 'sovereign,' that is, 'having the rights of the first-
born.'... That *first-born* means supreme in rank is confirmed
by what Paul says in the following verses. Jesus is the agent of
all creation (Colossians 1:16) and exists before all things
(1:17). He is not classed with the creatures but with the Cre-
ator" (Thomas L. Trevethan, *Our Joyful Confidence,* Downers
Grove, Ill.: InterVarsity, 1981, p. 37).

STUDY 3: THE DISCIPLE'S IDENTITY AND RESOURCES

Question 1. If you'd like, bring crayons and let group members
draw pictures with colors portraying how they think God views
them.

Question 5. "The latter part of [1 Peter 2:9] links with verses 5-
6 to stress the twofold ministry to which God's people are
called: offering spiritual sacrifices to God and declaring His
wonderful deeds.... Such a response, both Godward and man-
ward, will be natural and spontaneous when the Christian has
grasped that all these blessings spring directly from the free
grace and mercy of God" (*The New Bible Commentary:
Revised,* p. 1241).

Question 11. "Timothy was one of the first second-generation
Christians: He became a Christian not because an evangelist
preached a powerful sermon, but because his mother and
grandmother taught him the holy Scriptures when he was a

small child [2 Timothy 1:5]... Paul counseled Timothy to look to his past, and to hold to the basic teachings about Jesus that are eternally true" (*Life Application Bible,* Wheaton, Ill.: Tyndale, 1991, p. 2203).

Study 4: The Disciple's Standard of Greatness

Question 5. "Most businesses, organizations, and institutions measure greatness by high personal achievement. In Christ's kingdom, however, service is the way to get ahead.... Rather than seeking to have your needs met, look for ways that you can minister to the needs of others" (*Life Application Bible,* p. 1757).

Question 9. For the basis of Jesus' self-image, see John 13:3. For the basis of ours, see 1 Peter 2:9-10.

Study 5: A Disciple: John the Baptist

Question 4. Besides being thrown into prison, John was later beheaded at the request of Herod's stepdaughter. See Mark 6:14-29.

Question 5. Look especially at John 1:23,32-34. "He came to announce a new dispensation, proclaiming the advent of the kingdom of God...to prepare the people in intellect and heart for the reception of Christ...to point out the Christ in the person of Jesus...and to show the union of the two dispensations in the Christ, as the Lamb of God...and without jealousy he saw the fulfillment of his prediction" (John D. Davis, *Davis Dictionary of the Bible,* Grand Rapids: Baker, 1980, pp. 422-23).

Question 8. John's statement "may draw attention to the fact that John's disciples are giving him more supremacy than God intended.... Or it may express the divine authority of Jesus, which John could not take away" (*The New Bible Commentary: Revised,* p. 937).

Question 9. Review Luke 3:16-17 for a description of John's expectations about Jesus. Also, John was in prison at that time, with no hope of getting out—circumstances that could cause anyone to have doubts.

STUDY 6: THE DISCIPLE'S MOTIVATION AND MESSAGE

Question 2. Paul's fear of the Lord "denotes that reverential awe that should characterize the believer's life in view of his appearance before Christ as Judge" (*The Wycliffe Bible Commentary,* Chicago: Moody, 1962, p. 1271).

Question 7. "God brings us back to himself (reconciles us) by blotting out our sins...and making us righteous. We are no longer God's enemies, or strangers or foreigners to him, when we trust in Christ. Because we have been reconciled to God, we have the privilege of encouraging others to do the same, and thus we are those who have the 'ministry of reconciliation' " (*Life Application Bible,* p. 2099).

Question 9. The *American Heritage Dictionary* defines *ambassador* as "a diplomatic official of the highest rank appointed and accredited as representative in residence by one government to another."

Study 7: The Disciple's Values and Goals

Question 2. "The rite that [the Judaizers] advocated was no longer spiritually meaningful but a mere mutilation of the flesh.... There was a *true circumcision,* but it was not of the letter, but of the spirit (cf. Romans 2:27-29). It involved glorying in Jesus as the Christ, the Fulfiller of every institution of Judaism" (*The New Bible Commentary: Revised,* p. 1135).

Question 3. Paul was of the tribe of Benjamin, descendants of Jacob and Rachel. It was the tribe that produced Israel's first king, and it was known for bravery and skill in war. His reference to being a "Hebrew of Hebrews" indicated that Paul had Hebrew ancestry on both parents' sides. Also, he was a Hebrew, or an Aramaic-speaking as well as a Greek-speaking Jew.

Question 5. "No amount of lawkeeping, self-improvement, discipline, or religious effort can make us right with God. Righteousness comes only from God. We are made righteous... by trusting in Christ. He exchanges our sin and shortcomings for his complete righteousness" (*Life Application Bible,* p. 2151).

Question 8. E. M. Blaiklock writes of Jesus' death: "All that was of His humanity was crucified by His own hands, hours before the Roman nails, under the cypress trees in the Garden of Gethsemane. If a man can bring himself into conformity with His death, it is by imitation in feeble fashion of such utter self-surrender. Paul means that the spirit of the cross is to dominate his days, determine his conduct, and form his character" (*Prison in Rome,* Grand Rapids: Zondervan, 1964, p. 40.).

Question 11. See Acts 7:59–8:1 and 9:1-2 for information on Paul's former life.

STUDY 8: THE DISCIPLE'S INNER WARFARE

Question 5. Those who habitually do such things will not inherit the kingdom of God. "Paul is indicating that unbelievers habitually characterized by such deeds are not kingdom citizens" (John F. MacArthur, Jr., *Liberated for Life,* Ventura, Calif.: Regal, 1976, p. 110-11).

Question 8. John Stott comments: "We must not only take up our cross and walk with it, but actually see that the execution takes place. We are actually to take the flesh, our willful and wayward self, and (metaphorically speaking) nail it to the cross. This is Paul's graphic description of repentance, of turning our back on the old life of selfishness and sin, repudiating it finally and utterly" (*The Message of Galatians,* Downers Grove, Ill.: InterVarsity, 1968, p. 150).

Question 10. This is a daily decision of choosing to live under Christ's lordship, dying to ourselves.

Question 12. It might be helpful to give some specific examples of situations that might arise on the job; during coffee break; while driving; at home; when with a spouse, a friend, a child, or a parent; while watching television; or while reading.

STUDY 9: THE DISCIPLE'S OUTER STRUGGLES

Question 2. For an explanation of this *treasure,* see 2 Corinthians 4:1,6 and 5:18-19. Other translations use *earthen vessels* for *jars of clay* in the NIV. These two expressions lead us to picture something weak that is made from the earth (or created from the dust, as humans were) to hold something priceless.

Question 3. By this time, Paul had been mocked, imprisoned, beaten, and defamed. In fact, part of the reason Paul wrote the letter of 2 Corinthians was to defend himself against those who were twisting his words and slandering him.

STUDY 10: THE DISCIPLE'S RESPONSIBILITIES

Question 2. Not conforming to the world entails several things: "(1) We must realize that the present world system is evil.... (2) We must stand against the prevailing and popular forms of the spirit of this world, proclaiming instead the eternal truths and righteous standard of God's Word.... (3) We must despise what is evil, love what is righteous...and refuse to yield to the various types of worldliness surrounding the church.... (4) We must have our minds conformed to God's way of thinking.... We must have our plans and ambitions determined by heavenly and eternal truths, not by this evil, temporal and transient age" (*The Full Life Study Bible,* Grand Rapids: Zondervan, 1990, p. 316).

Question 4. "Healthy self-esteem is important because some of us think too little of ourselves; on the other hand, some of us overestimate ourselves. The key to an honest and accurate evaluation is knowing the basis of our self-worth—our identity in Christ.... Evaluating yourself by the worldly standards of success and achievement can cause you to think too much about your worth in the eyes of others and thus miss your true value in God's eyes" (*Life Application Bible,* p. 2050).

Question 9. Some believe that this section is not directed specifically toward Christians alone. Paul may have been outlining moral precepts for those outside the church, too—a kind of guide to community living.

Question 11. This passage concentrates on honoring and serving those around us, just as Jesus taught us. We can do this because God has created us all in his image and because each person is a brother or sister—or potential brother or sister—in Christ.

Study 11: A Disciple: Barnabas

Question 5. To see why these early Christians were afraid of Saul (Paul), read Acts 8–9.

Question 7. As Christians spread throughout the region, they went from preaching only to Jews to preaching the gospel to Greeks, too. This is the first time the gospel message was presented to the Gentiles. It was the first "missionary" effort, which was later carried on in Paul's and Barnabas's journeys.

Question 10. Note that Saul's name is changed to Paul in Acts 13:19. While Barnabas started out being mentioned first, he was, in a sense, demoted to being a companion of Paul.

Question 11. Barnabas's decision regarding John Mark was later vindicated by Paul. See Colossians 4:10-11 and 2 Timothy 4:11.

STUDY 12: THE DISCIPLE'S BASIC REQUIREMENT

Question 2. Since Peter had denied Jesus three times, Jesus may have had this in mind and wanted to encourage Peter. This special commission Jesus gave him was not only a test of Peter's love, but it also was a motivation and a delegation to take care of the church that was just beginning. Jesus questioned Peter the first two times using the Greek word for love, *agape,* a higher, broader-reaching love than any other. This unconditional love goes beyond affection, and it is the kind of love God has for us. The third time Jesus asked whether Peter loved him, he used the word *phileo,* the word that signifies a love for a friend or a family member. Interestingly enough, all three times Peter answered that he loved Jesus using the word *phileo.* It was as if Peter was saying, "Yes, Lord, I love you like a brother," while Jesus was saying, "I need you to love me as your Master first, and then I want you to love me as a friend."

What Should We Study Next?

T o help your group answer that question, we've listed the Fisherman studyguides by category so you can choose your next study.

TOPICAL STUDIES

Angels by Vinita Hampton Wright

Becoming Women of Purpose by Ruth Haley Barton

Building Your House on the Lord: Marriage and Parenthood by Steve and Dee Brestin

The Creative Heart of God: Living with Imagination by Ruth Goring

Discipleship: The Growing Christian's Lifestyle by James and Martha Reapsome

Doing Justice, Showing Mercy: Christian Actions in Today's World by Vinita Hampton Wright

Encouraging Others: Biblical Models for Caring by Lin Johnson

The End Times: Discovering What the Bible Says by E. Michael Rusten

Examining the Claims of Jesus by Dee Brestin

Friendship: Portraits in God's Family Album by Steve and Dee Brestin

The Fruit of the Spirit: Growing in Christian Character by Stuart Briscoe

Great Doctrines of the Bible by Stephen Board

Great Passages of the Bible by Carol Plueddemann

Great Prayers of the Bible by Carol Plueddemann

Growing Through Life's Challenges by James and Martha
Reapsome

Guidance & God's Will by Tom and Joan Stark

Heart Renewal: Finding Spiritual Refreshment by Ruth
Goring

Higher Ground: Steps Toward Christian Maturity by Steve
and Dee Brestin

*Images of Redemption: God's Unfolding Plan Through the
Bible* by Ruth Van Reken

Integrity: Character from the Inside Out by Ted Engstrom
and Robert Larson

Lifestyle Priorities by John White

Marriage: Learning from Couples in Scripture by R. Paul
and Gail Stevens

Miracles by Robbie Castleman

One Body, One Spirit: Building Relationships in the Church
by Dale and Sandy Larsen

The Parables of Jesus by Gladys Hunt

Parenting with Purpose and Grace by Alice Fryling

Prayer: Discovering What the Bible Says by Timothy Jones
and Jill Zook-Jones

The Prophets: God's Truth Tellers by Vinita Hampton
Wright

Proverbs and Parables: God's Wisdom for Living by Dee
Brestin

Satisfying Work: Christian Living from Nine to Five
by R. Paul Stevens and Gerry Schoberg

Senior Saints: Growing Older in God's Family by James and
Martha Reapsome

The Sermon on the Mount: The God Who Understands Me
by Gladys Hunt
Spiritual Gifts by Karen Dockrey
Spiritual Hunger: Filling Your Deepest Longings by Jim and
Carol Plueddemann
A Spiritual Legacy: Faith for the Next Generation by Chuck
and Winnie Christensen
Spiritual Warfare by A. Scott Moreau
The Ten Commandments: God's Rules for Living by Stuart
Briscoe
Ultimate Hope for Changing Times by Dale and Sandy
Larsen
Who Is God? by David P. Seemuth
Who Is Jesus? In His Own Words by Ruth Van Reken
Who Is the Holy Spirit? by Barbara Knuckles and Ruth Van
Reken
Wisdom for Today's Woman: Insights from Esther by Poppy
Smith
Witnesses to All the World: God's Heart for the Nations
by Jim and Carol Plueddemann
Women at Midlife: Embracing the Challenges by Jeanie
Miley
Worship: Discovering What Scripture Says by Larry Sibley

BIBLE BOOK STUDIES

Genesis: Walking with God by Margaret Fromer and
Sharrel Keyes
Exodus: God Our Deliverer by Dale and Sandy Larsen
Ruth: Relationships That Bring Life by Ruth Haley Barton

Ezra and Nehemiah: A Time to Rebuild by James Reapsome
(For Esther, see Topical Studies, *Wisdom for Today's Woman*)
Job: Trusting Through Trials by Ron Klug
Psalms: A Guide to Prayer and Praise by Ron Klug
Proverbs: Wisdom That Works by Vinita Hampton Wright
Ecclesiastes: A Time for Everything by Stephen Board
Song of Songs: A Dialogue of Intimacy by James Reapsome
Jeremiah: The Man and His Message by James Reapsome
Jonah, Habakkuk, and Malachi: Living Responsibly
 by Margaret Fromer and Sharrel Keyes
Matthew: People of the Kingdom by Larry Sibley
Mark: God in Action by Chuck and Winnie Christensen
Luke: Following Jesus by Sharrel Keyes
John: The Living Word by Whitney Kuniholm
Acts 1–12: God Moves in the Early Church by Chuck and
 Winnie Christensen
Acts 13–28, see *Paul* under Character Studies
Romans: The Christian Story by James Reapsome
1 Corinthians: Problems and Solutions in a Growing Church
 by Charles and Ann Hummel
Strengthened to Serve: 2 Corinthians by Jim and Carol
 Plueddemann
Galatians, Titus, and Philemon: Freedom in Christ
 by Whitney Kuniholm
Ephesians: Living in God's Household by Robert Baylis
Philippians: God's Guide to Joy by Ron Klug
Colossians: Focus on Christ by Luci Shaw
Letters to the Thessalonians by Margaret Fromer and
 Sharrel Keyes
Letters to Timothy: Discipleship in Action by Margaret
 Fromer and Sharrel Keyes

Hebrews: Foundations for Faith by Gladys Hunt

James: Faith in Action by Chuck and Winnie Christensen

1 and 2 Peter, Jude: Called for a Purpose by Steve and Dee Brestin

1, 2, and 3 John: How Should a Christian Live? by Dee Brestin

Revelation: The Lamb Who Is a Lion by Gladys Hunt

BIBLE CHARACTER STUDIES

Abraham: Model of Faith by James Reapsome

David: Man After God's Own Heart by Robbie Castleman

Elijah: Obedience in a Threatening World by Robbie Castleman

Great People of the Bible by Carol Plueddemann

King David: Trusting God for a Lifetime by Robbie Castleman

Men Like Us: Ordinary Men, Extraordinary God by Paul Heidebrecht and Ted Scheuermann

Moses: Encountering God by Greg Asimakoupoulos

Paul: Thirteenth Apostle (Acts 13–28) by Chuck and Winnie Christensen

Women Like Us: Wisdom for Today's Issues by Ruth Haley Barton

Women Who Achieved for God by Winnie Christensen

Women Who Believed God by Winnie Christensen